Racket

iUniverse books may be ordered through booksellers or by contacting:

iUniverse
1663 Liberty Drive
Bloomington, IN 47403
www.iuniverse.com
1-800-Authors (1-800-288-4677)

ISBN: 978-1-4401-0824-2 (pbk)
ISBN: 978-1-4401-0825-9 (ebk)

Printed in the United States of America

iUniverse rev. date: 03/12/2009

Racket

by Eric McCrossan

iUniverse, Inc.
New York   Bloomington

They say that if you need to explain poetry it's bad. But they do talk a lot of rubbish and who are they anyway? I often find reading poetry a strain as it takes a while to figure out what the subject matter is and, by the time I have, the poem's finished. I would not do that to you so I have therefore added a scene-setter to some of them to get the reader off to a start.

Cover photo : This is a drawing by Ulster artist Rita Duffy. It was used as a poster on a building project which was part of the Belfast Laganside redevelopment. The workmen cut a door in it – just visible in the photo – and added a padlock in an interesting position. Maybe it should be called "the invasion of the security conscious Goths". Most of the other photos in this book were taken in and around Belfast.

By Eric McCrossan

Introduction

I'm a poetry apprentice
my rhyming mouth is teething
taking an inventive trip
on seas of spirit seething

Building on the songs we sang
churning my lines; learning
how to put in rhyming slang
all of my life's yearning

If you think I made this stuff?
no; it writes me and you
in shaping it I learned enough
and hope that you might too

Let the poem suck the life from me
and put it on the page
so that others who can see
will understand the rage

Let the poem bleed the life from me
and spill it on the page
so that others who might see
can understand the rage.

1

Contents

Laugh until you die

Die laughing

You gotta laugh -
or the humour cops will get you.
Make your point and stick it in their eye.
For, you can be sad again tomorrow.
So laugh, laugh until you cry.

You gotta laugh -
or your friends will all forget you.
Have a stab, until the tears do come
Sad, to see your brow's deep furrow
Laugh, until crow's feet make home.

You gotta laugh -
or the rumour mill will hex you
Your leg hurts? Worry not the doctors scoff.
laugh, chase away the sorrow
So laugh, until your leg falls off.

You gotta laugh -
or the Government will sex you
Your report will hit the tabloid page.
In, the Sunday Sport - what horror!
Laugh, laughin's all the rage.

You gotta laugh -
Although your heart is heavy
Keep it light, make merry all you spy
For, all your time you borrow
So laugh, 'til you, with laughter, die.

---

shifty-moody

Sometimes life is ItchyTickly

And my thinking MuggyThickly

Often it's BurstyBubbly

a GolfShotWithWrongClubby

Some days I'm SuckUpThirsty

Others I'm all DamonHirsty

Known to be WormyWiggly

And it has been GirlyGiggly

Today, MyPoemsRhymyTimey

Tomorrow, FindingRhymesMeStymie

Some days I'm SocialTalky

Or maybe TakeTheDogAWalky

Now-and-then I'm JoggingReady

Or-then-again LieInMyBeddy

On good days, <u>Sir</u>PaulMccartney

On bad, <u>Mister</u>RingoStarkey

MoanAlone, TheWorldACursey

More oft' that, than CheekyChirpy

In canteens I'm PickyFoody

Do you think I'm ShiftyMoody?

Once Percy Ffrench wrote of an Irish innocent in London. How times have changed.

The City's Treats

Oh hear 'ye this woman's a wonderful sight
with the hip bones protruding by left and by right
and she don't "dig" potatoes, or barley or wheat
thanks to Atkins' advice she eats cold fatty meat
At last when I asked her that's what I could see
so I just took her hand, but this She was a He.
And for all that I found there that with which "she" pee
and 2 hairy legs sweeping down to the knee.

There's beautiful girls here, oh never you mind
and also some men from their nature resigned
Oedipus Complex, and Rosie's wet dream.
but let me remark things are not what they seem
And if that that Rosie you'd venture to sip
you'll both come away with a stain at the hip.
I'd go back to the bungalow waiting for me
And lock all the doors, get behind the settee.

I believe that when writin' you said you're impressed
As to how the fine "ladies" in question were dressed
well if you believe me, if ever you call
you won't find no breasts in those dresses at all.
I've seen them myself and it's half and half
as to if they're for real or just havin' a laugh
Don't go smokin' them hash pipes now Mary McCann
Don't you end up wantin' to dress like a man.

You'll remember young Lenny McGrillen of course
well he's over here but the voice, not so hoarse
I saw him today as she "cruised" on the Strand
Stopping the traffic with a flounce of the hand
And as I thought of the beard that's now gone
the local constabulary chose to look on -
But for all his great social life he'd rather be
with someone to love him and not pay a fee.

10

I know how space-time feels   (The Awakening)

They say it's the law of nature
that Gravity stays the same
at all times and in all places.
I fear they must be wrong.
Every morning
when I have to get up
I find that Gravity
(and its cousin Inertia)
increases 100 times
(but only once)
I think this is because
the terrifying racket of the alarm
rents the fabric of space-time.
I know how space-time feels!

Daybreak they call it
but it is the night that's broken
the day has gone and fixed itself
dammit I've just woken
Daymake I call it
the alarm clock has spoken
I stretch and groan and scratch-my-crotch
as an awake-I-am token

I try to kill the traitor clock
but it's putting up a fight
and tho' I choose to hit the "snooze"
the Sun turns on the light.
The light that yonder window breaks
It also breaks my heart
I've not slept all that it takes
and day starts with a start

Day fixed : night broke
the night has gone goodbyes
it's my fault, the day's fixed
'cause I opened up my eyes.

12

Snow Scene

It was, I remember, a kinder September
Then October burst on the scene
It rained, not a lot
November's not hot
December? That's where the snow's been!

The sound of one leg walking

All trips start with a single step!
But still 2 legs are needed
At the task of walking monopedal
Man never has succeeded

So trust me, as I know this much
Although it may be galling
The sound of one leg walking
Is the sound of one man falling

I pulled up behind a lorry carrying molasses and there was a warning sign on the rear "Non Hazardous Load" I was at a loss as to what I was supposed to do in response to this Hazard Warning.

Treacle Traffic

I saw a treacle lorry
driving down the road
the sign said, do not worry
"non-hazardous load"

I don't know why they said it
How should one take heed
of such advice? I read it
whilst driving at full speed ..

.. and braked too late to halt,
the anti-locking pistons
- icy road, devoid of salt -
still required more distance....

.... to stop my motor crashing
and the lorry I did whack
the treacle tap I'm bashing
with a resounding crack

and faecal looking treacle
came bleeding out the back
landed on my vehicle
and flooded o'er the track

''twas busy at that time of day
and so the load spread out
there and every which way
but smelled quite nice no doubt

though olfactively attractive
the treacle quickly set
I was stuck for hours in
traffic
in fact I'm toffee yet

the lorry stuck like putty
a truck "came unstuck" after
I was in a treacle butty
the butt of raucous laughter

If a lorry of molasses
(thixotropic, now you know)
on a motorway you passes
just mind how you go

treacle can't be trifled with
more risky than you'd think
you should not trust the
hieroglyph
when driving the Westlink

despite the early warning
that the lorry's safe to pass
it'll marmalise your morning
if you hit it up the ass.

Tantric Eating

I thought I'd try some Tantric Eating
Like that Sting from off the telly
tho' with him it's a sexual feating
with me its more strawberry jelly

You only do it once a week
just all week long - at table
I start with soup of spuds and leek
And stare 3 hours at my navel

Its a contemplative course is soup
if approached without baloney.
Oxtail enriched with Hoola Hoops
or sometimes Mulligatawny

I dissect each chunk of soupy stuff
and eat it with small tweezer
I find that three cuts is enough
I'm no secret carrot teaser

This Tantric thing is very slimming
as it takes so long to eat it
you can even do it while you're swimming
or whenever – you can't beat it

If the meal has peas it takes too long
as you eat them one by one
you pick them out with sharpened tong
and roll them round the tongue

Of course you are obliged to savour
every subtle hint of thyme
all the levels of food's flavour
or its such a waste of time

But here's a warning to the nation
If you get a food complex
from this obsessive concentration
Stop ! - instead try Tantric Sex.

One thing this thing is not is frantic
so you eat so little food
that the result of eating Tantric
is to lose much weight for good

But yet enjoy the eating of it
in truth that is just the point
you sit for days like wee Miss Moffett
chew curds and whey and a joint,

Lets hope not all the people try it
So the food manufacturer wishes
or the nation's total weekly diet
will be five loaves and 2 wee fishes.

Science

Evolution is likened to a River Out Of Eden. All rivers eventually meet the sea. Will it be like this?

The Sea of Eden's river

No sting in
the tail for
Which there is no cure today
we will endure
For now & ever and a day

We're all
perfection
and inscrutably nice
descended, evolved
generations up from mice

No worry
No hurry
We live for evermore
We've Reached
The Sea of Eden's River shore

Who was it
Discovered
how to cure decadence
Don't know; It was
A Million years since.

I've been told
sex was
for procreation once
making babies
What's that? I looked askance.

It's how humans
once started
They aren't needed any more
now that we've landed
The Sea of Eden's River shore

Once the
inventors
learned to cure mortality
babies were banned
in their totality.

But there were
protesters
"Women" wanted to give birth
How to give birth?
Don't ask me! There was no room on earth.

Maternal
instinct
They called it as they had no cure
we do now we're at
The Sea of Eden's River shore.

I think that
such a woman
was called "Suffragette"
as having babies
Involved some pain I bet

And so now
we know
how to prevent decay
That's why there's no "women"
living in the world today.

"Trust Nobody": says who?

Inside, the head of Man is dark
It is devoid of light
even Einstein
or Aristotle
So how do we know they were right.

All Man's thinking in the dark
No wonder that we fight
Even Newton
or Rasputin
And God knows they were bright

Which to trust is hard to judge
I don't know what to do
Even cynics
Say "Trust Nobody"
I say "Says who"

To many men of an uncertain age, such as I, comes the mans' condition that requires the doctor to do an internal. I read on the Internet that this was done by way of a "Digital Rectal Examination" What a relief I thought; a nice modern "digital" procedure presumably involving computers. It was the next day before I realised that mankind has always been digital having 10 of the little phalanges. It is :-

The Time Of Man

For it is the time of man
When nature's ruination
Is visited my body on
To exact recrimination

For being good; for being bad
Just for being there
She-Nature takes her aim at HE
That sits upon the chair

For that I'm asked to lie prostrate
For some prostatedigitation
The doctor dons the dreaded glove
For inside examination

For the passage of an instant
The moving finger wiggles
Against the one-way flow
And I suppress the giggles

For now it's time for a report
From this assault alimentary
A natural outcome flowing from
Unnatural rear entry

For mercy, mercy doctor please
Take off your safety glasses
Talk to me; what you have found
Are there any inner masses?

"For you the news I have is this
Your gland in size is ample
And in my view there is no need
For further test or sample"

For now I live, I do go on
And on and on again
I think I'll take, to celebrate,
A Norwegian cruise ship to Spain.

The Quantum Cafe

My local café, around the corner, has a round counter, around the which one queues to be served in a roundabout way in around three minutes. There is a sign as you approach stating "Queue both sides please".

Well I have tried but I somehow can't get the knack of queuing so that half of me goes to one side and half to the other or indeed, in a Quantum Mechanical sense, where all of me goes to both sides at the same time. At the same time, mind you, I do understand the principle - although they do say that if you think you understand Quantum Mechanics, you have gotten it wrong - the bastards.

This is a brave attempt to use Quantum Mechanics to overcome the Supermarket Queue Problem (SQP). This states that the longest queue in any supermarket will be the one that moves quickest. Therefore when you pick which queue to join on the basis that it is the shortest, you always get the one that takes longest. There is another version that states that the length of time a customer takes to be processed is inversely proportional to the volume of goods in the trolley but this version can be derived from the principal principle and so is rarely used in supermarket design circles.

If the supermarkets could adopt a Quantum Queuing Policy (QQP) this would be cured at-a-stroke, over-night and all-at-twice.

In the QQP one approaches the multi-queuing situation and, rather than using the Classic Queuing Strategy (CQS), one creates Entangled Trolleys (ET) and joins all the queues at once. You create as many ETs as there are queues; this is BO (Bleeding Obvious). When the first slot becomes free you become the next person and all the other entangled "you"s disappear. Their Wave Functions wave goodbye. You get served according to the order that customers arrive at the checkout area. Perfect. Does away with all the Quantum uncertainty.

Of course there is always the Murphy Conundrum (AKA the UpYoursSmartArs). As soon as the time comes for you to be served in the above way, the power fails and the operator you have picked turns out to be numerically dyslexic (dysproportionate?).

But I just can't work out how to split myself in two in my Quantum Café. Can you help? Don't all reply at once.

The Black Sun

The black Sun shines
in the black sky
We think it funny
We think it shy

What do we know of it
What do we care
how do we know it's not
Somewhere out there

Four by bloody four

Dear Lord we hate the 4X4
Auto box or 10 on the floor
In all their crass bull-bar-ity
I see only gross vul-gar-ity
The driver high looks down his nose
Looks down on me too I suppose
I hate them, hate them with a vengeance
Hate their size, hate their engines
No crumple zone to take the brunt
But a harsh, hard, hobnailed, high-set front
A rear to block the view for a mile
And an unforgettable lack of style
They're brutish, British/German barges
Driven by small-manhood chargers
Dear Lord we hate the 4X4
For all these reasons it abhor
But one thing above all others
For the band of hating brothers
The greatest reason we decry it
Is that we can't afford to buy it.

There once was a Gasworks near Donegal Pass in Belfast – now removed. The following is a fictional tale of what might have been.

Gasometer

Wendy Bow	Islamist	How we miss
Runs a Co.	Terrorist?	The usual hiss
Supplying gas	Intern	Gassy heat
Donegal Pass	& they'll learn	To warm feet
Belfast city	Say the DUP	And make tea
Gasometer	Inquiry	Reinstate?
Thermometer	And fiery	Replicate?
Goes up	Debate	Seems strange
Blows up	Illuminates	No change
Calamity	Eventually!	Despite atrocity
For kilometers	It was lightning!	The corporation
Manometers	It's frightening	Conservation
Go up	That much?	Despite odds
Flow up	Creates such	Of acts of Gods
Flattened city	Eventuality	Says gas 'twill be
All around	Ruination	Gasholder
Burnt ground	Recrimination	Behold her
Shock wave	MD	Go up
How grave	Wendy	Grow up
For society	Responsibility	Such a pity
Emergency	Resign, resign!	Titanic borough
Contingency	Redesign	Very thorough
First must	Facility	Defying God
Settle dust	Utility	With lightning rod
Alas alacrity	For you & me	And works committee.

For many years a "pretty Turquoise Blue boat" took daily a load of excess effluent from Belfast down the Lough to the sea where it unceremoniously "plopped in the ocean". The practice has recently stopped.

Old Stinky

Such men are they that crew her
Belfast's own maritime sewer
It's a city that is so demure
That it loads a blue boat with manure

And it's sent down the Lough to the sea
Where those flying fishes pee
Gamy it daily would float
The pretty turquoise blue boat

Any romance left in the ocean
Was ended for good by the notion
Which if not sad would be funny
Of using the sea as a dunny

I wonder what fate has in store
At the relevant distance from shore
For the merde determined to float
On being discharged from the boat

It comes from Whitehouse and Cultra
And is loaded aboard while still raw
Carrickfergus, Bangor, Millisle
Will eat it again in a while.

D.O.E. has now seen the crime
In polluting our sea with slime
Now the motion, no more in motion
No more to plop in the ocean

It's being recycled I'm sure
Into agricultural manure
But what fish have evolved in the water
Having been fed on the matter ...

..for so many years every day
And become addicted, dare say
And reached gargantuan size
Developing legs and thighs

Soon to emerge from the sea
To go looking for D.O.E.
Who recently failed to deliver
The produce of bowel and liver

Which it needs to survive and dive
Essential to keep it alive.
Will it travel up sewer and river?
Should we be paranoid and quiver??

Will it crawl up your anus and eat you???
Such a creature is bound to defeat you!
God help us if it chooses!!
To parasitize us and use us!!!

To feed it in its bathy home
Off the coast just off Ballyholme
Such an irony of evolution
Is our talent for making pollution.

Once Belfast was a major shipbuilding centre, building in great galvanized sheds, for example, the famous Titanic. Now there are "Titanic" boat tours on the main river - the Lagan - and the area once the Shipyard is the "Titanic Quarter" and an entertainment centre called the "Odyssey" Two large cranes called Sampson and Goliath remain and dominate the Belfast skyline. Titan; Odyssey; Sampson; Goliath. We're very big on the classics here.

Titans Bed

No more they paint the sheds galvanic
which once gave birth to great Titanic
no more the thuds of iron hammer
shout their rude staccato grammar
The "Shipyard" now just a "yard"
Employing just one man - a guard
Titan, has been "Quartered"
the ship sung, drawn and slaughtered
So big, so high, so very quiet
There stand Sampson and Goliath
(which one was the stronger?)
not "Quartered" yet - but how much longer?
What is this mythic hero worship
in this town of "Belfast", hero warship
Odysseus now has foothold
but are only one-way tickets sold
on Lagan tourist pleasure boats?
lets hope this one longer floats

The drawing office still extant
now draws tourists eyes askant
"Is that all?" But don't be sad
the building has a cute facade
so, I think, they will preserve it
so nice, I think it does deserve it
not a sign of where we're going
but where we were when we were growing
would we still be building Titan
if not for 30 years of fighting?

What next for the Titanic city
will tourists come and call us pretty
real cranes soon come back and steal
Connswater from the cranes of steel
real heroes make the city better?

We're famed for building peaceful walls
between the Shankill and the Falls
Famed for building ships that sink
that aren't as shipshape as you'd think.

An article in New Scientist Magazine reports that it has been discovered that there are more cells of E.Coli etc. in the gut of a human than there are (person) cells in the person's body. "The bacteria in our guts outnumber our own cells by nearly 10 to 1 - and nearly two thirds of them are unknown to science, new research finds New Scientist News - 23 April 2005"

Inside's Out

More micro flora cells en tota
in a body (says the Mag.)
than human cells; that's the quota
it's really such a drag

Hoisted by my own petard
The thought; it's such a loss!
outnumbered in my own back yard
I thought I was the boss.

But yet I am a democrat
and so I must be fair
give way to those cells of scat
which do this body share

More is more; less is less
There's more of them than me
And as we freemen do profess
The rule - majority

I might have known I'd be outdone
Outvoted by the stool
In proportion 9.9 to one
they the bosses; me the tool

So now I know the reason why
God made us. Deep inside
to manufacture E. Coli
and spread it far and wide.

Man On The Road to Hell?

(This is an undoctored photograph. In Spain "Sin" means that the
bus is "out of service" as we would say it, and "Man" maketh buses.)

The Tractor

It's the tractor factor
that soil compactor
taking the toil out of tilling
the soil

the prospect attractive
mankind hyperactive
taking its toll but still filling
a hole

machine maketh man
because machine can
taking us places by filling
our faces

the farm as factory
unsatisfactory
expanding our girth
as we're killing the earth

with practices pure
we might still endure.
are we making a plan for
when no more land ...

... or making a tractor
with a nuclear reactor
to watch water boil; oh the
saving on oil!

for tho' the world's round
it's finite & bound
are we serious or just
deleterious?

Imagine you are 4 years old and your only experience of apples is picking them off the shelves at Tesco; then you too might believe that-

Apples grow on the grocery shelf

Apples grow on the grocery shelf

I know this as I saw, myself

They grow at night when the shop is shut

All one size and perfect, but

They don't grow in a bag, like bread

They grow on plastic trays instead

I counted yesterday at four

today at five there were six more

They grew right on the shelf I'm sure

If they had not there would be fewer

And God lives in the shop's high roof

From where (s)he advertises soup

At a price that's "special, & fantastic"

(other's prices, "simply drastic")

They give all gain to charity

And tell you so, for clarity

So you believe the food is good

& their staff never ever rude

You can take stuff from the shelves at will

And give no money at the till

Just show them your credit card

To prove you're not Jean Luc Picard
I don't know why the cops don't act
I'm an accessory after the fact
just show them your chip & pin
To prove you're you, not kith or kin
& honest you, as is the prayer
On each bank note "I'll pay the bearer"
But pounds you never ever see
They don't exist - is it just me ...
... did you ever see one; ever feel it?

How on earth do people steal it
How to take what isn't there
And take it back to your evil lair
How to count it - it is virtual
It's a faith, it is spiritual
"I believe in the god of spending
God the Cent, and holy lending
The god of opening, non-stopping
The god of 24 hour shopping"
My mum says this shop is brill
The loyalty card discounts the bill
And my mum is a great believer
In any fiscal stress reliever
She's loyal to any shop that will
Give money back - "for that she'd kill"
Tho' I don't think she really would

'cos my mum's really, really good
Tho' "just you wait 'till we get home"
If I "don't leave my friend alone".
If I "hit him once", she'll "hit me twice"
Which I "won't find very nice"
'cos "hitting people's very wrong"
Unless you're old & big & strong
It's just as bad as making noise
Or trying to take apart your toys
But "a boy" I'm told "will be a boy"
Until the next time I annoy
I "should not be so moody or bold"
When she's in the mood to scold.

Doctor doctor

Doctor doctor, please feed me that potion
One more drop in that fathomless ocean
Of balms and creams and magical unction
Take as directed without compunction
Your obsession to keep me alive
Means I continue to thrive & survive
Having attained the great sum of years
half a millennium today; cheers!
Can you imagine in time long gone by
After 3 score & 10 you had to die
Praised be the doctors who had the insight
That since all illness could now be put right
The fate of our genes to wither away
As all imperfections forever stay
The wit of the genius who saw the solution
To the decay through evolution
Was to keep all men who were then alive
Not let them die but forever to strive
To preserve the last generation
The status quo in perpetuation
Safe at last from Darwin's clutches
We rely on medical crutches

Doctor doctor, please free up my motion
So I can plop without painful commotion
No spasms and screams or tragic contraction
Take as directed and attain relaxion
Your obsession will keep me sound
While I continue till my turn comes around
Having obtained after wait of some years
I have an appointment to get 2 new ears
Can you imagine in those days of yore
When organs wore out then you had no more
Rich be the doctors who had the great wit
They present the bills, could you now sign the chit
The state of our genius to while time away
As he keeps all change forever at bay

The wit of the genie who saw the solution
To the decay through evolution
Was to keep all men who were then alive
Not let them die but forever to strive
To preserve the last generation
The status quo in perpetuation
Safe at last from Darwin's clutches
We rely on medical crutches

The Sun is out to get you. One cannot possibly enjoy a holiday in the sunny
countries without girding oneself against the nasty rays.

The Palm Tree

The palm tree is my sundial
I chase its shadow all day
A frantic(!) attempt, if a trial,
To keep melanoma at bay

For my body is just far too spotty
To allow me to lie in the rays
So I must look after my botty
And shade it on hot sunny days

With a Factor of several hundred
Shadows are perfect for me
Which means that I am really scunnered
If I want to swim in the sea

So I tend to lie in a huddle
And I sleep 24/7
All except for a kiss and a cuddle
Oh yes this holiday's heaven.

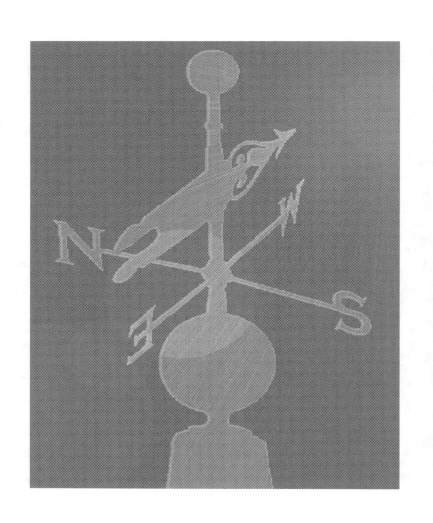

Religion

Who is the real hero – a Superman who can't feel pain, the soldier in the armoured car? Or the weak who persevere with life in impossible circumstances?

Worship heroes?

Supermen aren't heroes,
until they eat some dirt.
It's easy fighting villains,
if you know that it won't hurt.
If the one who hung on Calvary,
was a man and not divine,
greater was his courage,
to suffer for his time.

Do-gooders are heroes,
if they're doing it for love.
But if it's done for kudos,
for blessing from above?
Then it's a job for wages,
and a pension guarantee,
not so much to be admired,
as the ones who seek no fee.

Heroes built of granite,
fight for glory in the field,
feel no pain nor suffer,
they know not how to yield,
don't move me in the least,
or inspire me to the core,
as do solo crippled ladies,
Zimmer-walking to a store.

I see heroes all around me,
every day in street and town,
people facing problems,
instead of lying down,
They're heroes but don't know it,
won't be statues in the hall,
but the best of men,
and women, praise them all.

Who was the iconoclast in the 60s – Keith Richard or Cliff Richards??

Out Of The Shadows

"Yesterday"
"Way Back in the 1960's"
when "The Times They Are A-Changin'"
Everyone's a "Rebel Rebel"
They "say you want a revolution"
"You don't fool the children,
children of the revolution"
But "Who"
Who was the bravest
in this time of rebels

Cliff!
He was "King Of The World"
"Starman"
"Sitting on Top of the World"
But "Something Inside So Strong
"Me Myself I" "The Voice Within"
said you're "Only a Pawn in Their Game"
"You can go your own way"
"It's now or never"
"I'll do it My Way"
So he did "The thing you do for love"
"Shout" - "I believe" in the "Spirit In The Sky"
"I say a little prayer" to the "Sun King"
"He's hopelessly devoted to you"
and "I feel free"
"If I Ever Lose My Faith in You"
life would "Never Be the Same Again"
I'm "Putting All My Eggs in One Basket"
I'm not "Like a Rolling Stone"
I'm with the "Shiny Happy People"
"Jackie Wilson Said"
This is "Somethin' Stupid"
It's "Rock and Roll Suicide"

You'll be "Right Back Where We Started From"
You'll "be lonesome tonight"
"Here comes the flood"
There'll be "tears on his pillow"
In "Heartbreak hotel"
He's no "Wild Thing"
He's "Yesterday's man"
"Make It Easy On Yourself" - don't do It
You're "The Man With The Child In His Eyes"
and "Ain't that a shame"
You'll become "just another brick in the wall"
But "you never can tell"
"It Ain't Necessarily So"
He had "No Regrets"
"It's Still Rock And Roll To Me"
While REM are "Losing My Religion"
He became a "Phoenix From The Flames"
"Lucy In The Sky With Diamonds" "Loves Me Like a
Rock"
and "Love Changes Everything"!
He's "High Flying Adored"
Despite or because of "The Rhythm Of The Saints"
"Maybe I'm Amazed"
He could have just "Walk(ed) On By"
enjoyed "Whiskey in the Jar"
Now "Let Me Entertain You"
Post "millennium"
From "San Francisco" to " Rotterdam (or anywhere)"
"Ka-Ching!"
I say "Shine on You Crazy Diamond"
"Respect".

Church is I feel a bit limiting as you can only worship on a Sunday and only one God. Wouldn't it be better if -

Different Drums

I'm a man of all people and creeds,
staunch as a bundle of reeds
free in my thought, words and deeds
I'm planting, religiously, seeds.

On Sunday I A.M. to chapel
bless me for I am a sinner
transubstantiation I grapple
and go home to a great big hot dinner.

In the evening I go Presbyterian
"Free" of course; I live in Belfast
In Paisley's caress I can care again
and know that the feeling will last.

Monday is when I'm a Zen,
Buddhist that is, meditating
thinking in silence and then
doing some more contemplating.

Tuesday, to God's Prophet I pray
to Mecca, in respect, I do kneel
and my beard here is good I must say
my pale skin for to conceal.

On Wednesday I pray to Woden
as people once did long ago
and Pagans still him are a Lordin'
and Pagans are people who know.

On Thursday I'm once more a Viking
and they call me "Eric the Red"
my fair hair is much to their liking
and they're happy I'm easily led.

Friday is my day for Darwin
so my brain gets switched on for the night
his theory I find oh so charmin'
and I hope for God's sake that he's right.

For I'm ex'ed from the Exclusive Brethren
and my credit has long since expired
The Brethren class me as heathen
and the Masons black balled me - I'm fired!

If you do not believe in heaven
you can't go; all the writings foretell
but though you don't hold in heaven
you CAN still, I'm afraid, go to hell.

Saturday I turn to a new Jew
(sans surgery you understand)
And wishing shalom (how d'y'do)
to the few Jews who live in this land.

I'm a man of all peoples and creeds
and each day is my day of rest
I'm becoming well rested indeed
but my soul is as clean as the best.

I hope that they now don't invent
one more religion to borrow
or I'll give it all up for Lent
and Ramadan - starting tomorrow.

LIGHT

Make light your footprint on the world
Make light your guide to walking
Make slight your strain on others
Make love your aim when talking.

Supermonkey

They say 3 million people can't be wrong (except in China where it's 4 million) But seems to me 3m people must be wrong.

There's x million Jews, y million Arabs, Z million Christians, a billion Chinese (and whatever they believe) not to mention the Plymouth Brethren.

All believe something different. They can't all be right so if one is actually right the rest are wrong. Right?

If we're lucky it's the Chinese that's right. Yes, then the rest of us are wrong but there aren't so many wrong and collectively the Human Race isn't as stupid as if, say, the Jews are right.

My God! (or yours!!). What if the Plymouth Brethren are right!!! Then Humanity is really thick because 99.999% of us are wrong!!!! I told you not to mention the Plymouth Brethern.

I reckon that it's just a percentage game so lets call the whole thing "off".

Same

Imagine if we were all the same
No need for an ID or a name
As like as atoms in a gas
Of equal size and just as equal mass
No finger patterns for the cops to find
No other sort of folk; no other kind
Still human though - still homo wise
Just all identical in form and size
How would we act in this anonymity
How would life be and how society?
No lords no dukes no lower caste
The revolution has arrived at last
Egalitarian perfection
All one size and only one complexion
A brown, black shade of murky pinky yellow
Is your skin and so that of your fellow
What would be the point in talking
When all are just as clever as Steve Hawking
No point in sport e.g. football
As all the games would end up in one all
And if you lost contact with a pal
Then met up in the street or mall
How could you be ever sure
Of this conversational pursuer
That this person was whom he said
Or is a thief - or just druggy in the head
Better have no friends at all to savour
But treat every soul with equal favour
No point in passport photographs
No signature to write on bankers' drafts
With one faith there will be no wars
No country, armies or rebel cause
No need for anyone to rule us
Nor protect us from those who'd fool us
No guru to cure you of the blues
No Mensa; no criteria to use
No family to visit and to call
No need for society at all.

Man-Made God

Theology - the study
of how man made god
in his own image;
and why.
Man-made gods
of his imagination
and he himself worshiped.
In his imagination
he worshiped creation;
but missed.
We are god's sparrow,
Not his temple.
Yet even science
puts man at the top
of the tree of life
by default.

Thank God for GPS

Without Faith we are lost,
said God.
and Hope just makes a mess
But I find maps and compass
work
And there's always GPS.

Without Hope we are lost,
said God.
Faith is no success
And Charity is useless
Yes, I'd use GPS.

Without Charity we stink,
said God.
Hope is so hopeless
Faith, don't you think you
should
Thank God for GPS.

If Jesus came from Lisburn

If Jesus came from Lisburn
Wasn't exotic,
nor quixotic
and the gory story
Wasn't tragic
nor magic
Would we believe just the
same?
++++++++++++
If he was called Joe Quinlan
Not foreign -
from Old Warren
And for schooling
Went to Tonagh
with sister, Bronagh
Would it be such a wholly
shame?
++++++++++++
Would it be hard for us to hail
Him
As our saviour,
when He's our neighbour
Vocal but local
Seen jogging
or walk-the-dogging
All around Wallace Demesne
++++++++++++
If Jesus came to Lisburn
Wasn't labelled
nor fabled
and the glory story
tried to present here

in the leisure centre
Would he go down in the hall of
fame?
++++++++++++
If He worked on the Avon
stand in Boots
And He spoke
like Lisburn folk
(sometimes told a joke)
And no son et lumiere
From this perfumier
Would he impress & have
hoardes to tame
++++++++++++
And if those feet in modern
times
Walked Batchelor's Walk
Talked Distillery talk
And built a new jakuzi
Or worked in Green's
A pleasant lad
Would we agree that He had
"came"
++++++++++++
Can we see God in Lisburn
Not yesterday
Nor far away
And restore the story
Down to earth
No virgin birth?
If not it would be such a
shame.

Stand Tall

Stand tall - Look down on none
Die for the cause - Never to kill one

Love yourself - Love your lover
Embrace her - Never smother

Need loved - Need more to love
Be a lion - With a soul of dove

Be proud - After the fall
Want much - Take nought at all

Give much - Free of all cost
Given thus - It is not lost

The Worm's Turn

Take a worm; thicken the skin
(so to keep the moisture in)
Then give it the means to talk.
Next add some sticks of chalk.
Out of 2 sticks make an arm
So it can fight & do some harm.
Out of 2 more then a leg
So it can rise and food to beg.
Then watch out as the worm turns
Into a man and scripture learns
And then upon the world to squirm
Until once more it turn to worm.
The imprint that is left is bone
And perhaps a partner left alone.
No more, we souls who still endure,
About that worm will know for sure.

Skin & Parts

Am i no more than skin and parts?
A synthesis, protein with hormone
No more than a file in the doctor's bag
Thus circumscribed, defined

Am i "expecting"? So the test imparts?
A new person will visit, when grown
No more a child, am i bearing one now
Thus consummated; primed.

Am i just born, a product of hearts?
Label "mccrossan, m, half a stone"
No more mum pregnant, does the tummy sag
"He's adorable", women find

Am i just baby food and farts?
Wetting the babygrow, on a mat prone
Growing so quick, as days elapse
And circumcised? Never mind!

Am i just one more left in "Rug Rats"?
A parent's priority, getting on
No more than a car commuter in line
So congested, daily grind

Am i a teenager, spotty, with warts?
Heir to the world i think i own
No more dependent on anyone else
Thus confident, maligned

Am i the food, tea & jam tarts?
That potent brew, with cherry scone
From good food, accrued, comme d'habitude
Thus consumed, combined

Am i consumer of gin and arts?
A poker dealer or play trombone
No more than notes for playing "rag"
Thus syncopated, unrefined

Am i computer, bus, UARTs?
Processor person, an IBM clone
No more than a file on drive C: or G:
Thus categorised, outlined

Am i ageing? As the frailty starts?
Grandchildren will visit, when grown
No more in my prime, am i "bearing up well"
Thus soft-soaped, declined

Am i CAT scanned, laid on the carts?
A positive; problem; Treatment Zone
No more than a year or 2 at best
Thus forewarned, road signed

Am i no more? Then kin departs
A plot in cemetery, with headstone
No more than script on the stone inscribed
Thus en-graved, reclined

Am i no more when skin departs?
Am i no more than remaining bone
Everything else to earth returned
Thus to dust am i consigned?

Was I no more than a flight of darts?
Through time flying having been thrown
Did I hit the bullseye, or double 13
I know not - am I mankind.

Grandads

God made grandads lazy so the house might not be clean
and when grandwee'ns visit the stor will not be seen

God made grandads crazy so they can still be fun
despite the fact they're lazy and incapable of 'run'

God made grandads hazy so they forget a lot
such as then, when Bill or Ben broke the flower pot

And God to grandads says He make sure the house is fit
long may grandad's days be and long grandad will sit.

This would just about fit on my gravestone.

No Material I

Now that I am immaterial
residing on the plain ethereal
pursuant to a walk funereal

This last song I did propose
to advertise me in repose
as in time I decompose

no more to flatter or to flirt
impeded as I am by dirt
Dressed at last in my last shirt

No one to see this sight sartorial
Instead let this be my memorial
This happy soul is post-laborial.

Heaven's Below

Heaven, as you know, is aquatic
to be found in the eastern Adriatic
in between both Greece and Rome
where civilization came from the foam

came from heaven at the word of god
(who was, at that time, in the form of a cod) {see
later}
to try to sort out all the land
which then was nothing but trees and sand

the attempt I regret was only to falter
and we have been the devil to alter
by god they tried but the cod we fried
was the holy cod who now has died

So Man has been below indicted
for crimes of woe we have been cited
The indictment read by a Barracuda
such a fish as there are none shrewder

Sturgeon asked for quid pro quo
"we want their skin - they took our roe"
"they think they are made in the image of god
but yet they wield the fishing rod"

"fish don't cry so by and by
it's cool to watch them suffer and die
or throw them back to suffer more
from recreational fishers ashore

"we have sent Mankind such blessing
but they have such a knack for messing
They would turn gold bars to lead
free power into nuclear war instead"

For every boon, they make a bug
But yet these creatures are so smug
They think that they are number one
Of all the beasts that see the sun

It suits them to forget that we
Who live in heaven 'neath the sea
Have been here some billion ages
before they came in the final stages

"they are more selfish than any shellfish
more randomly vicious than a jel'fish
if they're allowed to go unfettered
we creatures of sea will live to regret it"

From Auschwitz to Beslan, Belfast, Dunblane
Ethiopan famine (they blame on the rain)
Nagasaki firestorm nuclear furore
(Hiroshima such a show that they did it once more)

6 million souls from the east shores of Med
Got in the way, so they ended up dead
2 towers felled, still with people inside
3 years have gone now & tears never dried

They spend much more on "weapons"(*) of "battle"(*)
Than producing food and tending their cattle
These concepts (*) unknown to us here below
some things it's better for us not to know

Can't you see the way it's heading
Man the means to Armageddon
They dissect & kill & carry the gun
They hunt, do you hear, not for food but for "fun"

They kill their own over politics
And pollute heaven with their oily slicks
no redeeming feature for sure
They are the problem we are the cure

The trial has now taken place
we were argued for by plaice
"they know not what they do" he said
but before the verdict he was dead

caught in the nets of fishers of fish
and sold in a pub as a special dish
the fishers did not understand
his pleas as they brought him in to land

they just thought he was having a fit
and so they thought nothing of it
as they sung an Irish shanty
unaware of their folly sailed back to Bantry

Plaice was replaced by a panel of dace
well qualified to defend human race
and they tried, even cried, but alas also fried
plucked from the court and removed from the tide

And so the fate of man was sealed
by god - now a walrus, who's gun wounds have healed
{sea creatures take it in turns to rule -
the whales excused as they are in school}

The verdict was read by the lord privy seal
to the lawyers, who mostly were eel
"all kinds of human are forever damned
bring them to me but bring them canned"

My advice to you reader is show acumen
if you go to heaven don't say you were human
or St Peter the Great at the gate (a skate)
will redirect you to the fiery grate

Pretend you're a pig or a rat or a vole
or god-the-swimmer will swallow you whole
your chance of pleading a defence is sunk
you'd be safer to make believe you're a skunk

The human race has been rejected
and god is feeling quite dejected
that he (now a shark) got it so wrong
and Man, off the mark, as it says in the song

The song the sirens sing, summer long
"come to me Man, you know you belong
in the sea here with me, don't bother to plea
god is hungry and wants YOU for tea"

One in the Eye

Standing by the road was I

                     I must have drawn god's ire on me

A puddle; vicar passing by

                  And (S)He drenched me in irony.

Just imagine if it were your job to hang around outside venues in the hope of getting a "flash" photograph of a female celeb getting out of the low slung car in their high slung skirt.

NickerClickers

Do the PaperRats, those HappySnappers,
those dogs of phowr, sssault their subjects with HerAssMent?

ASBO? what could be more A.S.
except maybe B.O. This PeepingTomfoolery, Mysoginist Cruelty

By comparison with the BushWhackers
Porn makers shine. are paragons. Their Ladies volunteer

If the NickerClickers tried to photo me
I'd thwart their kinky; wear a mirror up-skirt
flash the flashers
so they could see them selves
in the Mirror, (Sun and Star)
as indeed they do now.

Time and again a man or men somewhere stretch our notion of how low a
man can go. In 2001 it was "a leader unknown" - O.B.L. His aim appeared
to be to topple the world by aiming at the top. It worked with the building
but surely not for the world itself (having aimed at the top nation.)

From the Top

It couldn't happen
You've got it askew
Men won't, just on word from the top
the selfish genome
will make them eschew
they won't die for nothing; they'd stop

You can't be suggesting
don't be absurd
a building collapse from the roof
you must hit the basement
I give you my word
with maths I could show you the proof

How could a people
of sophistication
be abused by their leader unknown.
Contra United Nations?
they don't make invasion
but fall from above like a stone

The world is too big
The UN too strong
To ever get caught on the hop
You do not belong
Your aim is so wrong
The world won't collapse from the top.

9/11

Ring 911 –
the World Trade's
falling
with urgency.
Insurgency
emergency

Ring 9/11 –
the day that hell
came calling
people dying
more crying
no planes flying

On 9/11 –
who went to
heaven?
Who can tell?
Many heavens;
one hell.

The Tunnel Of Words

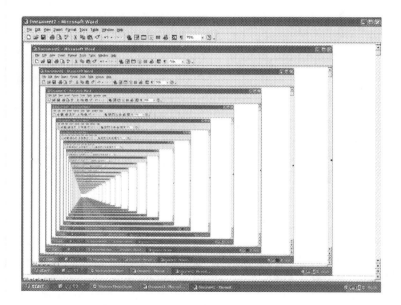

Words

The thing about fiction is

It never happened
maybe couldn't
maybe shouldn't
but, never happened
not in that way
not as they say

Not true at all
never happened
superfluous
incongruous
waffle - to baffle
but - never happened
not in that way
not as they say

The thing about
fiction
it looks like
it happened
in that way
as they say
2 million people
can't belong
to the cretin's throng
can they?
can it happen?
in that way?
I say! I say!

Am I the sticking
point; am I?
could that happen
that me so shy
would be the guy
to see through
the fog of flannel
on every channel
"reality" in wide-
screen
telly-V
is hardly ever seen
should this happen?
in this way
every day
this false pretending
this neverending
belief suspending
Also the movies
that happened
but not in that way
but as in a play
its all pretend
in the end
its all Columbo
mumbo jumbo
divertisment
with advertisement
(which also never
happened
not in that way)

And soaps
build up hopes
for voyeurs
they make it legal
to spy on neighbours
its up-skirt drama
Is Eastenders
the end of us?
good as we get?

The Bible,the
Koran,The Tora
etcetera
did it happen
as the say
in that way
in that day
maybe not
dare I say

If you are what you
eat
are you what you
watch?
this doleful diet
of quiet and riot
do we buy it
and then maybe try
it
will it then happen
in the same way
just as they say
how will we pay
how we will pay!

The graffiti in NI is somewhat formulaic and often features an expression which they spell out in full but I will abbreviate - "F.T.P." Where the "P" lives in a large palace in Rome.

The Word on the Street

Are all loyalists gay
For they are wont to say
"FTP"; goodness me; don't you see
Do they find him OK
In a queer kind of way
What a twist in the tail; well flip me!!

Such brotherly love
Is a gift from above
A boon ecumenicalistic
No more boxing glove
When tug comes to shove
But a hug and a session holistic

Thanks be to god
The Orange is odd
And desires this carnal communion

Say yes to the prod
Yes give them the nod
And blessed be the State of the Union

And so it has been
With the orange and green
Since the era of queen Nefertiti
You know what they mean
And it's easily seen
That the word on the street is graffiti.

Fires cannot create, only destroy, but nevertheless the young of Northern Ireland are keeping their flame alive for the cause. The future's bright; the future's Orange. The fires burn on 11 July and are followed by the Orange marches on the 12th. Until quite recently the main constituent of the fires was used tyres and wooden pallets. The use of tyres is now banned. The fires are a spectacular sight even before they are lit, on one occasion featuring on the front page of the Times.

Keepers of the Flame

Dioxins laughing in their tyres
await the night in pallet spires
As looking down on neighbourhood
teenaged experts Kingly stood
to build, to burn in fact and mind
a message seared, a world defined
Down through many years, the same;
they are the keepers of the flame

The history of teachers – spurned
was never learnt as this was - burned
Down the ages; down and down,
both in country & in town
Passed insidious and deep,
thus we will maintain, will keep
In territorial declaim
by the keepers of the flame

Not Costa suntan brown and rich
but bonfire fire-burn red and kitsch
It fades to Orange in a day
for one more year destined to stay
Inside, tho' clear for all to see
"We are the people" and will be
Because our heritage the same
as the keepers of the flame

Do tourists brave the streets of fire
to marvel at the rude attire
And Party Songs, and wonder how,
EC rules we disavow
How industrious they strive,
how terraced houses do survive.
And what it is that they proclaim,
Ulster's keepers of the flame.

Tick Tock

What is it that we take from rhyme?
That prose deposed in tick tock time
It seems to have the power to daze
And turn us with its slick, quick ways
When all it has to offer over
Normal-speak is bossanova;
Tempo, just entertainment
To distract from what the brain meant

And thoughts in other tongues presented
No longer rhyme or chime contented
And so mean less to folks not local
Whether read in bed, or vocal
And thoughts in other times composed
Often are not well transposed
Into our modern speaking fashion
Or resonate with present passion ….

… so might mislead although unwitting
I hope we will not be forgetting
That just because a story's choral
Does not prove the moral moral
And tho' it scans it does not follow
That the writer's brain box isn't hollow.
So if you hold that this is true
I'd ignore the above if I were you.

Some people seem to believe that the way to look clever is to use long words no matter who their audience is. In the case of a general circulation this actually displays a distinct lack of intelligence as communicating is all about being understood.

Free (vb) Speech (n)

O' come whilst I tell you a story
If such is your idea of glory -
to coin a long phrase,
and to hide in the haze,
of words quare and obfuscatory.

Plain speaking's not just for a dummy
or for dealing with baby by mummy.
It's for communication
throughout the nation;
it's so rare but when heard it's so yummy.

If you're stuck for a word - don't despair,
for the dictionary's plenty to spare.
So please don't invent 'em,
you'll only repent 'em,
as your thoughts travel over plebs hair.

I'd like to speak in favour of cliché

I'd like to speak in favour of cliché
The antis for too long have held full sway
Hip Hip Hooray for cliché is what I say
Carpe Diem, hold up your head cliché.

Neologism, if the only thing allowed
would mean you'd hear little babble from a crowd
in bar rooms or in night clubs, music loud
would be needed to disguise the lack of rowd'.

Being anti's hackneyed, don't you think?
Complaints to me are just a waste of ink
I'm a hard man from the markets and I drink
And cliché is the cup with which I clink.

Conversation consternation would ensue
I hope my gist that you don't misconstrue
Cliché holds the world as one like glue
Life would be sterile if you can't say, "I love you".

Come on cliché make a comeback for it's time
linguistic fascists must confess the crime.
But wait - this poem is an idea sublime.
Its very freshness is the death knell of this rhyme.

———————————————————————

Those carpet bombers of retailing are computer literate but can't always aim their cold steel, or is it gold steal, as accurately as might be called for.

A Comedie of Spammers

In the kind word of Spam   if your sex life is iffy
they can make you a man   and do so in a jiffy
they'll improve your allure   and you know for sure

you'll seldom be stuck for a stiffy.

Oh the kindness of Spam   their concern for your coming
the noblest of Man   and so good for your plumbing
they'll implore you to spend   and your money to send

you will be so hot you're humming.

It's a kind of a fiddle   is this world of good deeds
and to me it's a riddle   how they know all your needs
they say I need length   and an increase in strength

for the wide propagation of seeds ......

....but I am a person   on the w rong (?) side of fifty
and my seed for despersin'   no longer so nifty
If I acted the young buck,   If indeed I know my luck

I'd be thrown in a home for the shifty.

If you find all this Spam   Unsolicited selling
As I do, a Scam   And you just feel like yelling
As your in-box gets longer   And your ang-er grows stronger

just thank God for a natural swelling.

70

I said "Ice Head" she said

It was a Monday night or Tuesday. It was a muggy night in Tucon.
Visibility was down to 90 million miles. We hoped it would improve
so that we could see the Sun. How come you never see the Sun in
the Mirror? Is it like Vampires? No; nobody likes Vampires.

A knock came on the door. It was a mess. Amess came in.
Another knock. It was easy to see how. Come in
Easy, said How. "How", "Easy", "Amess"; could happen! How easy a
mess could happen too. It happened to me.
It happened two times.

Amess was heavily armed. And the legs too. And the back was a
sight. So I built a hotel on it without delay and
without planning permission - or should that be "an" Hotel - no it
was a 'ospital. I named the 'ospital Bedside Manor. The right
front door was entrancing. The other one was exciting. Down at
the old Pull and Push. I was in the 'ospital getting my NI
contributions back on the drip. Nurses attended to most of my
needs. The nurses came in shifts. Would you put your life, or
anything else, in the hands of shifty people. I did and I'm here to
prove it, or maybe improve it.

The immigrant doctor logged on the computer. With the second
swing of his immigrant log the computer broke into
pieces. Actually maybe it was an adze - no it **was** a computer. The
immigrant doctor struggled to pick up the pieces -
he was very depressed. He was black-balled of course. I think he
got off light. Get off the light I said. Don't you
call me "Ice Head" he said. "I'm a section 75". That's nothing I
said; I'm a caesarian section. I told you not to call
me "Ice Head" he said. I said I'd call him later and he seemed
happy with that.

I went to the canteen & asked for an Irish ham salad with no Mayo
but extra Sligo to make up for the lack of Mayo. Yum yum -
Michael Jambon does taste good between 2 heels, between you and

me. Michael was off - on, on, on he waffled – what a Ham. A cheesy ham waffle – lovely. I queued and then chewed the lewd, rude food when I could, and should, have eschewed – how I rue the chew. Hubble bubble, tummy trouble; at the double, toilet rubble. I ran. A bad smell followed me. I ran quicker but still it followed after. After food poisoning. The hospital was pseud but the salmonella was real enough. I took advice from my Indian Uncle Satis. His surname is "Factory" - he's an industrial relation – ("Satis Factory" - could happen) He used to be a Shoshone shoe shine boy but now he shines at sycophancy. He said the cooker was liable. It was an Aga farrago.

The cook was Mr Kuk. He started life working in a sea food shop called The Prawnbroker. He decided that he didn't have the patience to work with crustaceans and succumbed to nominative determinism. I took the Kuk to court. His service was OK but he sliced his backhand. That looks sore I said. "Salt & Vinegar" he said - but it sounded like "sore finger". No bloody wonder, I thought, and it sounded like silence. The court ruled in my favour - 2 parallel lines it was – still every little helps. I didn't know what the Judge meant with his judgment. As he read it I lost my way. Then, he read it out loud. Thi(it)nk. I lost my money, my shirt, my temper, 1 stone in weight and the will to live (although I still have the Will to die for).

I still can't see the Sun - Visibility still 90m.

Four Fifty Years is a long time. For 50 years I hadn't seen the sun until I fell in love with the sky. He took me places I thought I'd never be. Kidnapping I think it's called. This guy's bad news. Eventually he got fed up and exploded from obesity. That was the end of the bad news; here is the bad weather forecast "might rain might snow – who knows".

And now the football results :-

Old Newtonians 1 : Albert Einstein 2 (After extra time)
(Isaac sent off for standing on the shoulders of giants)
Darwin 1 ("ID"- Own Goal): American Creationists 0

God The Father 1 : God the son 2
God The Holy Ghost 3 : The Red Devils 616
QPR 3 : QCD An infinity of speckled Rabbits
Quantum Entanglement 1: Quantum Entanglement 0
Quantum Entanglement 0: Quantum Entanglement 1 etc
Reading 4 (Fun) : Leeds 2 (Knowledge)
Bolt On 2 : Hearts 1 (Transplant)
Chelsea 0 ; Rushden and Diamonds 12 (McCrossan 12)
And in the periodic table there was just one match
Hydrogen 1 : Helium 2.

I escaped from the sky. To celebrate my escape I went to the
Tucon Opera House. The safety curtain fell on me. It was
premature but not underweight. Life is so unfair. They say that in
50 years there'll be no fair people at all. So who will man the
coconut shy? And as for the wishing – well!

They sent for the first Aida but it was no use so they got the
second one. That was the end of me; the curtain fall was my
curtain call. I took a bow. I took my leave. When the leave was
used up I came back to work. I was sick off work, now I'm sick of
work. So there I was playing Devil's Advocate on the trumpet
voluntarily. But the Devil won by a short horn. He was sharp; I
was flat. But we had a bet and there was the Devil to Pay. It was
a contract made in bad faith - Satanism. I sold my sole to the
Devil so he had the upper hand. "Keep the change" said the Devil.
I kept the uppers.

I wondered, (sic), sick, down the street, looking for all the world.
"My name's Electric Bill" said the tart. "You turn me
on". "My friends call me Billie but you can call me daily". "Do you
want some business?" So I sold her shares in Shorts. We turned
into a car park and turned into a couple. The car park notice said
"Private Park" – "perfect" said Bill. I took off my Shorts & parked
my Rover. Then I paid "The Bill". The wages of sin are tax-free.
"Euro?" I said. "No I've got a bad back" she said. She gave me a
receipt. She gave me clap - I must have been good - they don't
usually applaud. I went to Doctor Dick Doherty, a clever-dick
Doctor, who said he could fix me up with a nurse, but it would cost

extra.

But I fell for Bill. It hurt. From now on you can fall for yourself I said.
"Don't call me 'ice head'" she said. "I got this head from my father before me."
"Your father had to be before you - he couldn't be after you."
"If he knew what I did at night he would be after me." "He used to be a church Elder - his name is Berry".
(Elder "Berry" - could happen!)
"That makes you 'Billie Berry'."
"No my dad and mum made me - don't you know nothing?"
"That's a double negative".
"Don't you talk about my parents like that".
"Ice head", I said. "Its an oxymoron that's all."
Then she hit me.

Billie was actually christened "Chastity"! She remained chaste until the lady chest arrived and then she was chased. She was chastised for exhibiting her vast chest in an uninhibited manner. Its just a chest she said but the jest was not appreciated. Her aunt, Cedent, (aunty "Cedent" - could happen) said "I suggest you conceal the best of your chest or your vest will be a mess". Nevertheless she professed to impress the rest of the nest and wore even less. I must confess the stress of this testiness was the start of her progress from knitting to knocking - but that's just a guess. "What's the biggest number of customers you've "had" in a night Ice Head?" I said. "144" she said. "God that's gross" I said. She said I'd be perfect in a small part in a porn movie – at least that's what I think the gesture meant.

Our affair lasted for many minutes. Four many minutes. Too many minutes. To many that is not long but then you
haven't met Electric Bill. Did you meter? Would you admit it?
Did she? Did she charge? Are you AC or DC? Do you
have a standing order with Electric Bill - or do you lie. Come clean.
Anyway, I'm positive our relationship is terminal.
The spark has gone. She's old currency. She's not the current one.

I still can't see the "Current Bun" - Visibility still 90m.

Once, Electric Bill had decided to go straight. Once Electric Bill had decided to go straight, she went straight, to a Nunnery, and changed her name to "Other". She put on a paradigm shift. "Does my Gluteus look maximal in this?" she said. It was the time of The Inquisition - 4:30 – or maybe it was 5:30 – something hurty anyway. She worked her way to the top, which was a pleasant change for her being more of a bottom-up sort of person. Then she decided to become a heretic - just to stretch herself. (Other wise!) But it wasn't working, lying on the Rack all day and lying on her back on the Rack all day wasn't working. She didn't want to be left on the shelf. Who would? But Hu was Chinese, not a Christian, and so not eligible to be tortured. Other was given a job in the sewing room - habit forming? Has anybody ever seen a nun get out of the habit? None have. No doubt a Nun has.

But old habits are hard to dye. Bill went back on the street. She had always walked that way having been a backward child. She bummed around awhile and drifted backwards into the backstage at the Tucon Opera House. She realized it was a play on words otherwise it would have been mime. She ordered a drink from the barman Phil M'Glass. Unable to see her way clear to look where she was going, she it was who made the curtain fall on me; it was Nun Other. Out of remorse and out of money she went back on the game and scored straight away. She bought a Jack Russell, bitch, and called it "Jane Russell" though it looked nothing like her.

I never saw the Sun that muggy night in Tucon but I saw stars on the stage.

Fonetix

No more will I wory unduly
of the spelcheker dynamix
I wil becum truly unruly
I am going to turn to fonetiks

To hell with the dam duble L's
I'l spel words as I chouzes
They wil not rool me again
those U's and asperate Q'ses

And I'll vary the wurds as I go
As long as the sens is intact
I'l cense that and go with the flo
In a sence, as a mater of fakt

If **people** can't read it, its sick
Its rong not the pepple - kno this -
If werds can't be red by dislexick
Not them, but the lexia that's dis

So in future all riting that's writ
Shud have to pas just one test
Must mean something to evry bit
Of man; lecksicks and the rest

Ps why is there not - or is?
A program to take txt as above
And output what's meant, à la Liz
(Queen's English) now that I wood luv

Spell Checker - my part in its downfall

Their ours homewards offing leash
Datsun durst hood awl rite
butter of tense pelt a rye
hand parse thee chequers buy.

People

Now that we have labour saving gadgets for all tasks, we need to deliberately "exercise".

Slow jogging

The jogger runs so slowly
those feet they hardly shift.
The arches they are lowly.
Perhaps she wants a lift.

Is it "run" or walking
And not so very fast
Got no time for talking
Is she running from the past ...

... or running to tomorrow?
For what does she hope?
Is she sick, in sorrow
or can she just not cope?

A typist on a sickie,
seems no doubt to me,
be better as a brickie,
get exercise for free.

Jogging gets you nowhere
you've not already been.
Run here to there to here
demoralise the spleen.

Jug'lar's bulge and pulse race
on ancient paving cobbles.
Nike SportsBra just-in-case
Jiggle, jogg'n woman wobbles.

Jogger jogging more slowly
Not on sportstrack fast revolv'n.
Does she think of ideas holy?
as she life's fitness puzzle's solv'n.

The jogger's fading –
Should she halt?
"Half way home;
more to tax-me.
Pass the chip shop?
Pass the salt !!
Got the mobile,
phone for taxi"

Moon Walker?

I'm driving the car to the exercise centre
Take the lift; use self-open doors as I enter
I'm building an Ozone shaped hole in my life
I'm married for sure but I don't have a wife
The fertility doctor will build us a son
whose life in-vitro has already begun
I warm up the coals so to cool down the beer
To enjoy cold winter nights with good cheer
I cool down the car so to warm up the earth
And break all those bridges-I've-burnt, with my girth
I'm a man of tradition on the road to perdition
I'm Homo Economicus and I'm on a mission
Greed be my Motto (I call it "success")
If needs be, the lotto might fund my excess
I am alive in this time of such plenty
but I have to ask - "incidentally"
"Oh lucky am I but will it end soon?
Or if you can't stand the heat can you go to the
moon?"

After The Fall Is Over

There's no such thing as free-fall the price is just deferred
until the fall is over and your personage interred

6 feet deep and 6 too wide but feet to walk no more
no pomp or circumstance After the fall is o'er

Delight at eating fatty foods only descends to girth
and a broken back for mourners as the carry you to earth

There's no such thing as free-fall where gravity holds sway
when the fall is over there in the ground you stay

and money spent but never earned just interest accrues
and your will is good for lawyers but all but they will lose

There's no such thing as free-fall the price is paid some day
when the fall is over the bank will find a way

Intoxicants can get you high from where the falls begin
though you think you're going upwards and die with a manic
grin

There's no such thing as free-fall the price of getting high
is to gyrate over, over as you tumble through the sky

There's no such thing as free-fall the price is just deferred
until the fall is over and your personage interred

6 feet deep and 6 too wide but feet to walk no more
no pomp or circumstance. After the fall is o'er

Faces off

There is a Spike shaped hole in the ground
now that the Milligan's gone.
God, how we laughed,
our faces off.
Then we laughed again with them on.

Name this child

Name   : Eric
Nationality   : Irish-Ulster-Scots.
Religion   : Non-Subscribing Unitarian
Football team : United
Qualifications : As follows :-

Few understand the idea of statehood
As those like me who have a choice
I can be Irish or I can be British
I can exercise my demographic voice.

Few comprehend the notions of religion
Like those with the God-given right to pick
Protestant, Jew or dissenter
or non-subscribing catholic.

Which of these I am ascribed to
is just an accident of birth
like coming out the wrong orifice
or birthing in the Solway Firth.

There should be an Internet site
to which we login postnatally
and study all the complications
for 18 years at Bill Gates' knee.

And then we have to make a decision
as to which side we belong.
Whether natural born or cloned
pick wisely, don't you get it wrong.

Will I be a Jewish Catholic
Hungarian Hindu or sceptic Yank
Will I live in the world's great cities
or in the country with a septic tank.

Will I hold Saturday precious
or make Sunday the sacred cow.
Oh put me down as undecided
For I still can't make my mind up now.

They say the test of your allegiance
is the football team that you cheer on
It's not where you earn your living
Surrey, Singapore or Saigon.

In the UK it's difficult for natives
never mind for the immigrant
To decide who to cheer on
or the tongue in which the name to rant

If your mother was a Walloon born in Watford
and you father was an Ulster Scott
and you were born in Swansea
do you cheer Belgium, one or the whole bloody lot.

Which makes it hard on the terrace
where do you stand what do you wear
if you get it wrong you'll be in trouble
but whatever, don't say that you don't care.

Or everyone will just conclude
that you're Al Quaeda on a job.
and they will all gang up for once
and you'll be torn apart by the United (sic) mob.

If you're not with us you are against us
say the Christian sects to the other ones
you go to hell, and us to heaven
in the end, at last when Kingdom Comes.

Listen Man you are my brother
kept apart only by the 6 degrees
we are one, you are not other
I know you won't you know me please.

Name   : Man,
Nationality   : Man,
Religion   : Man,
Football team : 11 men,
Qualifications : None.

Now we have become destroyers of worlds by remote control – and it is so easy to do :

E.G. went over the sea (The Heroes of Hiroshima)

Echo Golf went over the sea.
Over the top. On the moral high
the pilots, who would not see
the pain as foreign children fry.
so efficiently, so instigatedly,
so indiscriminately, so incineratedly.

Gayely they flew, the few,
"Never in the field", 'till then,"
"of human infamy" had 2
dozen killed so many men,
so efficiently, so instigatedly,
so indiscriminately, so incineratedly.

"God's on my side" said they
But God has never said so, still.
He wrote so much, so why not say
Heaven welcomes those who kill
so efficiently. so instigatedly,
so indiscriminately, so incineratedly.

That plane never landed
it's flying still
looking for millions more
children to kill
Their confidence flying
so high above 'til
they decide on the target
re-start the drill
so efficiently, so instigatedly,
so indiscriminately: and so incinerate me.

My life

My life
Born Fife
To dad's wife
Caesarian knife
Strife
Was rife

My life
Played fife
Took wife
Constant strife
Took knife
Slice slice

Cut twice
Not nice
A vice
My life!
Paid price
Got life

The Woebegon Court

Part I - The Court Sits

"In the Sovereign State of Woebegon
The County of Hardlesson
This Court sits to write (sic) all wrong
& stands for nil transgressin' ..."

.. said the clerk in style of herebefore
And it came as no surprise
As Stout processed, overdressed
When he then said "all rise"

Judge and jury, Stout & crew
The best of man's allotting
The Sinner, sitting - starts to chew!!
Stands for crimes most rotten.

Stout sits on sack of woolly thought
Dispensing wit and sense
Knows as only judges ought
Honi soit qui mal i pense

"Bring forth los hombres Woebegon
All persons here accused
Of practices profane. Anon
They shall not be excused"

So here before judge Stout today
You're facing malediction
He'll let the pleader have his say
Then punish with conviction

"How do you plead" - (oh by the way
Thanks for the employment
Due to so much crime today
I live in Great Enjoyment)

Part II - The Plea

"In the Sovereign State of Woebegon
The County of Ardlesson
The people versus me? Case on!
For I'll not be confessin' "

"In the sorry State I find myself"
Said the chewer I foremention
"I can but choose to plead the twelfth
Amendment to convention"

"In the Sovereign State of Woebegon
The law has tests of truth
The State must, with doubt beyond
Put forward all the proof"

"Before we start this carnival
This Woebegon antiquity
J' Accuse all those carnal
Of complaisance with iniquity"

"Where is the <u>proof</u> that Woebegon
That State that's far from Perfect
Has a right to try my case forlorn
And execute the verdict"

"What man, or men of Woebegon
Can show me proof preemptory
Of their right to sit upon
A fellow man, contemporary"

"This right that Woebegon would say
Might come, they claim, from God.
The Almighty is not here today
Which I find almighty odd"

"This woebegone democracy
I did not choose to rule me

To try me, fry me, crucify me
Or in religion school me"

Part III - The Verdict

The jury's fury, stout & true
The breast of man's a beating
The Sinner sitting - stares to you!
"<u>He</u> stands for crimes of cheating"!!

In that we know he did the acta
So why filibuster
She's no more virgo intacta
He surely did accost her

The verdict ready, Stout and crew
 Process again most regal
The jury comes back 2 by 2
To make the process legal

The wives of fishermen and others
Watch with scant concern
Sitting, knitting, baby-covers
Les tricoteurs moderne

"In the Sovereign State of Woebegon
The Townland of Muchardour
You and your double did conjoin
To make our task much harder"

"As herebefore declared in law
This is a crime most awful
What the honest witness saw
Never could be lawful"

"Here, before Judge Stout you stand
In bother much embroiled
12 men, my crew, I now demand

If _he_ that girl despoiled"

"I ask the jury, stout & true
To tell us the conclusion
The Sinner's fate depends on you
Let there be no illusion"

Foreman Touman clears his mouth
He's ready to proclaim
In the name of good men north & south
"_He_'ll have to take the blame"

Part IV - The Sentence

"For the Sovereign State of Woebegon
The County of Ardlesson
This Court finds that you did wrong
& stands for nil transgressin' "

"To answer for this deed malign
You must be put inside
It's just by chance & not design
That the victim has not died"

The case earned notoriety
As a test for evil crimes
And was studied by society
When reported in The Times

It also served to write 4 songs
Sung by Simon & Garfunkel
In the Soccer Ground of Woebegon
A monstrous old carbuncle

Part V - The Appeal of Exile

On appeal to a higher power
The Sinner was successful
& went to live in Alandafar
Where he finds life less stressful

In the Sovereign State of Alandafar
In a house he calls Dunchagging
He whiles away time at the bar
And often is seen bragging ..

.. of how he licked old Woebegon
That arrogant confection
Stout & crew, sine qua non,
Poor woebegone protection.

Gone but Not Forgotten I

Blessed would be a man who could forget
And yet recall that which he wishes to, and when
To put aside all things that cause regret
Yet trade fond memories with the rest of men

Just consider if a means you could devise
So that you could forget, at will, that which you knew
Of books once read that cannot then surprise
So you could read them, many times anew

But yet recite, when needed, quotes from all of them
Quiz questions to make you a millionaire
Get looks of admiration from all men
(Yet for popularity have little care).

And those that pain you - the hurt you can put by
It cannot touch, if you don't want it to
Never more can it make you cry
You are an island, a rock, never blue

But recall each moment, every day of pleasure
That you ever had with that friend, now turned
To an enemy, cruel past all measure
And get wiser from the lessons learned

Is memory "friend" or just a hollow sham
If we could treat it like a servant when <u>we</u> say
Access it like computer RAM
And turn it off if it gets in the way

Blessed I am not, I can't forget
Memory rules me as it wishes to and then
Will put before me things that make me fret
Yet bids fond memories never come again.

Gone but Not Forgotten II

(Eric's eulogy on the inhabitants of an Irish graveyard)

Here lies my friend, to die no more
There stands the wife, who did adore
And I have time to look around
This deadly fascinating holy ground.

(No ploughman wends his weary way
Ploughmen never weary get today
The tractor drivers' union says "no way"
And gets them leave in autumn on full pay)

Look at the size of your man's obelisks
He must have been a big shot, took risks
He is big in the totem department
Now that from this life he is apart bent

And this one lies in a bed of roses
Under a flower shower reposes
Would you look at the buds on that
Must have lived with auspicious éclat

An Italian battalion, Irish now,
The pizza-pasta-trade bade "ciao"
Passport Photos on the headstone shown
As to how they looked when kin & bone

(In case you think this a racist stance
I know they don't all work in restaurants
But all of those now living (?) in Killinchy
Do; although descendants of Da Vinci)

And flowers wilt in sympathy
No plastic cheaters here you see
In this Irish field of plotters
Murphys, Sadies and McTrotters

(Despite the best attentions of the colour men
I don't believe "all Catholics are the same"
The plots to which above, below refer
Are graveyard plots, their earthy share.)

Here a papist plot; there a Morman
Ryans, Lu, Chang & Gorman
In this ante-room of heavens
The faiths laid out in 6 and 7s

No ghettos here; no point !
At the last we are as humans joint
No postcode for our rest address
Just obelisks to other folk impress.

(But please don't think their lives a waste
We live, we do, we die and off we haste
We play a part of which the world is needy
The big, the small, the thin, the fat, the seedy

Do not think it better only, living
At the top of all and to be great things giving
The value of each man is to achieve
A life well lived with others, I believe)

The House of Lisburn Man

Lisburn is all in his house
Bow Street left to cat & mouse
Essential goods in vital store
Now not needed any more
Assistants shirk, rest & pray
On a quiet evening late Sunday.
As Sun condescends to night.
In only picture-takers sight
Does the light that is in rain
Twinkle in the photo-brain.
Reality of Bow Street lost
On Lisburn - home and tossed
On chaise; long; before TV
To watch Alternative Reality
While I take time to my own
and watch the real Sun down
alone
As I stroll content along
By Market Square where once a
throng
Passed me by and saw me not
When we were Lisburn's daytime
lot
Only one more person there
In Sunday's evening Market
Square

Though in crowds some hours
before
The same 2 persons each ignore
Now we have to form a view
You on me; me on you
And wonder as we wander past
Should one acknowledge or let
pass
What will the other think or do
If I nod, or greeting I eschew
As when but 2 are in a lift
To speak or not-that is my drift
Such an everyday decision
Not discussed on Television
Dilemma comes to lots we cast
Who speaks first-who the last
Hello says he; hello I say
And so we pass; that time of
day.
Lisburn looks as cities do
When empty save for one or two
When Lisburn is in his house
Lisburn man and Lisburn spouse
It's they who make the city play
When Moon condescends to day.
& shutters clatter out of sight
To banish loneliness & night.

Symbolism

She's an international "babe" a lady,
THE International Lady maybe,
Called Po or Jo or Jill or Glenda.
A circle with a cross appended.
Sometimes, in the family circle
This lady can be known as Myrtle
For me she always will be "SHE"
As she plays her part in families' tree.

She needs a friend, this gal symbolic
With whom now and then to frolic
A roundish person, male with arrow
Pointer, sword, banana, marrow
A hunter and a gatherer
Electric shave or latherer
Or maybe a shave decliner
Thinking hairy faces finer
A circle too and equal size
But the body round is mostly eyes
He has for Myrtle (Jo and Sadie
Any plus-appended lady)

Banana chewing HE would sally
Along the promenade and alley
And act the Joe DiMagio
And think of il seraglio,
(whatever science teachers say)
50,000 times a day,
(whatever pompous preachers pray)
At work at walk or talk or play.

SHE struts the streets with plus apparent
Dressed to please in come-on garment
"less is more" the paradigm
In advertising the plus sign.
The more SHE walks and talks and wiggles
The more HE stalks and gawps and giggles.

They're getting on and on and closer,
The risks HE takes are getting grosser
And as the bonds of friendship strengthen
So does the sword of virtue lengthen
So he takes his courage in his hand
As he decides to make a stand

"I hope you will not be offended,
O' circle with the plus appended,
If in this part I praise your parts
Which I appraised right from the start
I've scanned you, you custard tart
I put you in my shopping cart
On Internet and supermart.
I love your parts with all my heart.
I really think that we should start
Plus means more to me than life
And I want you to be my wife"

And so the circles go together
Circulating "L" for leather
And that's what makes the world go round
And the escalator up and down.

Here is a thought for girl and man
Whilst they're post-coital drinking
If yin and yang were Dot and Dan
There'd be be no need for thinking.

My wife has had a form of cancer for many years so we spend a lot of time in hospitals. One place that we became very familiar with was the Bridgewater Suite of the Belfast City Hospital, the cancer outpatients centre.

Bridge over troubled water

We're pending in the room for waiting
The doctor's words anticipating
Suspending normal social chitter
Hoping he can make us fitter
No bandage, no badinage
No "pity me", just rage au cage
Just waiting, waiting patiently
And glad the doctors charge no fee
To hear the verdict of the testing
Is it a curse or then a blessing
And a description of prescription
based on the CatScan depiction
After being here for weeks
A voice at last within me speaks
"All roads lead from womb to coffin
Interspersed with sneeze and coughin'
This bed a lay-by on the route
And though it's not a jolly hoot
We're living in this time we borrow
And life must not be spent in sorrow
The doctors' pills provide extension
A longer path from pram to pension
And though the road is sometimes bumpy
Your lymph nodes, or your bowel, lumpy
The blessings that disease uncovers
To those who fail or who recovers
Are greater than the tests of treating
We are the fate-of-mankind cheating
For all with providence must play
Soon or later, none can say
And every day that you find pleasure
God considers priceless treasure"

Mi Hollydaze

For my holidays we went to the Kanary Islands. The Canary Islands are named after a big yellow dog which is the same colour as the bananas that grow there. You eat bananas but not dogs except when they are hot. I don't know if dogs eat bananas but they probably do if somebody peels them for them.

It is warm there even in January because of all the volcanoes. The rocks on the Canaries are ignorant. One of the islands is going to fall into the sea due to global harming and chew Nami America. I asked daddy if we could watch but he said no - it wasn't part of our package.

The Canaries are on the Continental shelf. My aunt Annie, who came with us, is on the shelf too but I am not allowed to say that to her. She doesn't know, I think.

Ladies in the Canaries are poor as they can't afford the whole bikini. They mostly just buy the bottom half to save money. They don't use the braziers. Because they don't have any support for their chests they have to lie down all day. The men lie down too to keep them company. They don't have jobs so they have plenty of time.

Everybody lives in blocks of apartments with a big swimming pool at the back. The apartments have showers so that the people can see what rain is like.

We went to the Canary Islands on a big bus that showed films of the sea in all the windows. Mummy said it was called a nairyplain but it said Airbus on the side. Mummy's friend Ethel moved house to the Canaries when she got tired – I don't know how she got the house in the nairyplain 'cos we were only allowed one suitcase each.

You have to have fun on a holiday even if you don't want to. Mummy said it would be a sin not to with all the money it cost. We had £1,500 worth of fun. Fun there is the same as anywhere else but warmer.

The local people are called the Canaries. They all speak English or German. We went to see a mountain which my daddy says the Canaries call Hell but I thought it was OK. Well, for a mountain anyway.

Daddy threatened to take us to the Canary Islands again next year but only if I was good.

Eric McCrossan   Primary 2   Age 56$\frac{3}{4}$

Canarian Sunset

An old man and Old Lady
beside themselves, with tea
sit a while reflecting on
the change from land to sea

Old hand and handmaiden
together gathered here
harboured they upon that wall
to 'count their days of cheer

Pater Familia and Queen
have seen the sun go round
grandchildren aged X-teen
yet, count their teeth, so sound

In days of old a man for gold
set forth this harbour from
Cave Canary, they might say,
that he sent to kingdom come

But this old man and lady
plan no such a ploy
the mater simply is afraid
he no longer is a boy

And how much longer can
they reside beside the sea
woe betide the day to come
that two no more will be

For one and one makes life
and all that which we do
and one man and his wife
beside themselves with glue

In such a scene there is a lot
of what we are and what we're not
that which some may not recall
 not for a day; or not at all.

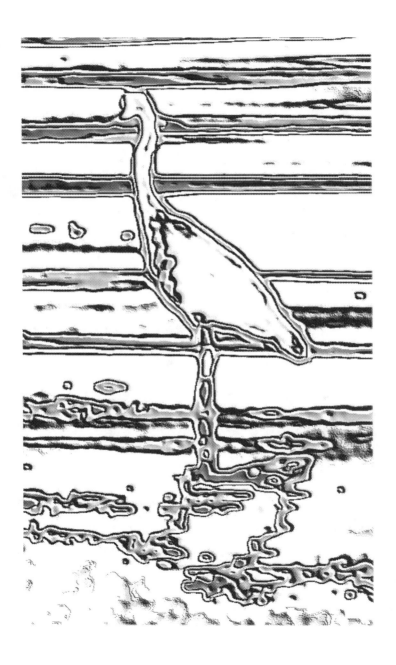

The Animal Kingdom

The Parrot Nation.

I wish I was a parrot, for
they don't spend their time
wondering how to win the war
Or how to tackle crime.

The parrot nation's happy
just being who they be
why oh why; why oh why;
why oh why aren't we.

The Parrot rules the roost
Without recourse to law
(Tho' some might need a boost
When dealing with Macaw)

Parrots don't use shops
Of themselves they trust
and they don't pay cops
To keep 'em safe from lust.

Are you more likely to be injured by a rat or a swan? I suggest that it is the latter as you would give a rat a wide berth. This phenomenon is widespread in the animal kingdom.

Swan Song

It's so slight and sassy, like a Spice Girls release
but keep half an eye on the Come-To-Play Beast.
It stalks o'er the land, looks out over the sea
and the "B" very near was the finish of me.
I'm here to advise you, I'm ConsumerLine,
the Beast will enthral you and ask you to dine.
It will deceive to flatter and natter and natter
But the lull of its chatter and the rhythm's what matter.
Not the words or the meaning or the text or the sub-
but the hypnotic movements it makes with its gub.

Beware boys the Beast called Come-To-Play
and watch your back so a wise man did say.
It may have no bark but its bite is so deep.
OK, it's not fierce, but its morals are cheap.
It will sucker you in and there is no doubt.
It will watch as you burn but not put you out.
The eyes are green but they're outlined in black
as a warning to all men; its best to keep back.
It's a warning of which I should have took heed
of the "B" my Glutei Maximi bleed.

Once you're dispatched by the Come-To-Play
there is no kickback, you've had your satay.
Its heart isn't black (!) tho', it hasn't a care,
for there is no sign of <u>any</u> heart there.
It can live very well on the blood of its prey,
Cette jolie Bête noire de "Aller Jouer".
There are cosmetic products that Beasts hide behind.
They look almost human and they act almost kind
'till they have you in range and you bite on the lure....
The most dangerous creature can look so demure!

Come-To-Plays thrive in this world, I know - now.
It only takes one - one that knows how
and the biggest will tumble will rot and roll
as the Beast makes light of your life and your soul.
The riskiest venture is the one seems risk-free
and a treacherous place is the realm of the "B".
If you think evil's ugly, and Satan's obese,
you are wrong - the Devil's this Beast.
Don't mark the book 'til the last page at least.
Deceit is the art of the Come-To-Play Beast.

The short memory of the butterfly

Do caterpillars looking at a butt-er-fly
as that flutter-go-lightly stutters by
complain of that flighty never-do-dwell
I'd never behave like that, bloody hell

as the young man looks at grandaddy long leg
the cranium, for all the world like an egg
what a funny concoction of age and decline
bet he wished he had hair just like mine

or butterfly look down on the cater-pill-ar?
That branch-upon-crawler who'll never get far
no ambition to reach for the heights
will never see, as I do, such sights

as the old man looking at sprackley youth
such a concoction of spunk and uncouth
"not in my day"; and "I wonder why"
I never did" and "won't, by and by"

Poor butt-er-fly; his memory so brief;
poor cater-pill-ar; can't see past a leaf
It's just as well that man is complex.
Thank you good Lord for cerebral cortex.

Relationships

The I Love woman

The Isle of Woman's a triangle
same degrees at every point
pleasure, pain there entangle
and couples 'come together, joint
man and woman come, together joint.

The start, the end of everyman
Won't eat, but has an appetite
Toys with you, just because it can.
No teeth, but will engulf you in the night
Nor will it give in without a fight

Who dares to interrupt with coitus
This riddle that could easy eat us
Nevertheless you'll make a fuss
Of this site-to-be-hold that will defeat us
The story-to-be-told ends in a foetus.

Isle of Lady answer if you can
can you conceive, a better plan
I will forever be your fan
Even though you call me Desperate Dan
Isle of Woman please say Isle of Man.

PS
I'm sitting in a diner
writing this, on a vagina
I wonder what the other eaters think
Of the wierdy beardy lot
With the face that time forgot
eyes light up sometimes and then put down his drink.

Do they see me as a nutter?
As I juggle with the butter
Or a secret, seedy paedophile at bay
If only they could see

The Pocket PC on my knee
"Coitus interruptus" !! they would say.

Some would simply smile
Some would "the lot" revile
& they would call the manager or fight
but the man reading the Sun
Would think it all such fun
what his paper has inspired me to write.

The roar of the cock.

Hear the lion crow,
the cock roar,
see birds swim
and fish soar.
It made such a difference,
when you said that me you adore.

Since you came,
the cock roars.
Since you swam
to my shore,
and walked to me differently.
I'll not forget what you wore.

See my heart glow,
the cock roared,
senses swam,
me floored,
by you, such a different buzz
than I've ever been busied before.

Stay with me.
I'm cock sure
We are twin
at the core
"us" such a different tale
tu sont toujour mon amour.

Let the world go,
the cock roar.
Let us swim,
evermore,
bare in the indifferent sea
of the world outside of our door.

The Wind

In my winter, northern town
It's a scene I must put down
In photo-words therefore to show.
Sun low, heats slow, no glow
A cold-wave comes heavy clouded
Upon a street with persons crowded
Making loose-scarfed walkers scurry
Seeking warm they hurry, flurry
Subject to the wind's disposure
Terrified to face exposure
Hair wind-ruffled; (people too)
They scuttle onwards fro & to
To the sanctuary at last
Of The City Hospital Belfast
Where lies the wounded Citizen
Warded women; wards for men
Safe from winter wind & weather
Getting well or worse together.
So many senses form a team
To make me realize this scene.
In one second it comprises
What I know & some surprises.
I've come to see my patient wife
who struggles on the edge of life
But has more of life than me
And shelters me within the lea
As cold I comes, heavy treading
through crowds on streets, bad news dreading
I, a loose limbed walker, stagger
Seeking warm but showing swagger
My mind ruffled; (spirit too)
I shuttle daily, as you do,
Subject to the mind's displeasure
Alone & cold in equal measure
To the sanctuary so vast
Of The City Hospital Belfast
Where lies one half of who I am.
If I am hog then she is ham.

The Conversation.

THERE ONLY ARE 2 NORMAL MEN
MY FRIEND, THAT'S YE AND ME
UNTIL WE TALK A WHILE & THEN
I'M NOT SO SURE OF THEE

IT'S HARD TO FATHOM OTHER FOLK
THEIR ALIEN PROCLIVITY
AS HARD TO UNDERSTAND, I JOKE
AS THAT THEORY "relativity"

AN UNEASY BALANCE WE MAINTAIN
ONCE WE HAVE DRIED OUR MOTHER
FROM JOHN TO JOE THERE IS A STRAIN
BETWEEN ONE AND ANOTHER

FROM THE TRIBE TO WHICH WE DO "BELONG"
THE HOBBIES THAT WE FAVOUR
AND THE SPORTING TEAM WE CHEER IN SONG
AND WHO WE CALL OUR "SAVIOUR"

THE LINES ARE DRAWN IN SANDS OF TIME
LOTS CAST FOR WHAT WE "OWN"
SWORDS ARE DRAWN TO "FIGHT FOR MINE"
LINES OF BLOOD ON SKIN AND BONE

THERE'S NO 2 WAYS ABOUT IT, SON
MY FRIEND, THERE'S YE, THERE'S ME
ALTHOUGH WE TALK AS IF WE'RE ONE
I'M SURE OF ONLY ME.

Apollo and Me

I'm bored
I've had all that I **can** take
This life is a **mis**take
It's tiresome for **God's** sake
Oh what a **heart**ache
My yin & yang **will** break
This world it takes **the** cake
No better than **a** fake
I'll jump into **the** lake
What difference would **it** make
It won't be an **earth**quake
It will not the **dead** wake

I'm bored
I'm really dis**gust**ed
My fortitude **bust**ed
My custard is **crust**ed
It's all done & **dust**ed
My teddy is **just** Ed
The wind it has **gust**ed
For love I have **lust**ed
But relations have **rust**ed
Me not having **sussed** it
I just was not **trust**ed
So to rancuor it **thus** led

I'm bored
How did it **go** wrong
We loved for **so** long
Then she said "**so** long"
For me the bells **ding** dong
I'm no longer **King** Kong
Life is no **sing** song
And she had such a **cute** thong
But spoke with a **diphth**ong
Which just sounded **so** wrong
Did not seem to **be**long

It clashed like a **brass** gong
When it makes a **bing** bong
Now she's gone to **Hong** Kong
A journey that's **so** long
And she's playing **ping** pong
At which she is **quite** strong
Protected by **the** Tong
And engaged to one **Tom** Wong

And I'm bored
Feel I'm on **the** rack
And there is no **way** back
Now I've got **the** sack
It's alas and alack
And my life on a **new** track
As I face up to **the** flack
And try not **to** crack
But "hope", I **do** lack
I've had my last **barm**brack
There's no Jill for **this** Jack
So what do you **think** Mac
I do not have **the** knack
I might just as **well** pack
All of my **knick**nacks
Put them in **a** sack
Change to a **new** tack
I just cannot **this** hack
This will be my **last** quack

For I'm bored
The TV is **rout**ine
All programmes **foreseen**
No point in the **damn** screen
"Everywhere" - **I've** been
I'm venting off **my** spleen
It is not a **good** scene
To see me in **this** mien
But it is an **old** theme
When a man who has **been** keen

118

And thought her a **real** queen
Finds there'll be **no** team
And knows just what **that** mean
His number is **thir**teen
He is in **be**tween
The cops and a **shi**been
I load the magazine
Of a gun, sub-**ma**chine
And blows off my **head**, clean.

I'm - **dead** - bored
No more the **clip** clop
Of horses as **they** trot
Killed by the **one** shot ...
...but lucky I **for**got
In my su**icide** plot
To include in **the** pot
Bullets - what **a** prat
Ergo the **shot** floppt
And dead in fact **I'm** not
Due to the **floppt** shot
Well aint that **a** riot
Should'a used para**quat**
So I lay down in **my** cot
Into the **cot** floppt
At midnight on **the** dot
I am such an idiot
A bloody in**sane** sot
I don't care **a** jot
The world can go **to** pot
Yes Claude I'm **a** clot
No Sir Wal**ter** Scott
Misery **my** lot
I shouldn-a-been **be**got
And whilst not a **big**ot
Nor ever a **des**pot
I feel like a **ro**bot
As I lie here on **my** bot
Succeed I **cann**ot

119

I'm wet as a **pee**pot
And this is the **up**shot
If for a **harl**ot
You have a **soft** spot
If you are a **zea**lot
Your ardour is **white** hot
You dopey **ma**ggot
You ropey **fa**ggot
You sour Lance**l**ot
You white Hot**ten**tot
You concrete-**hulled** yacht
You excuse for **dry** rot
You Lankashire **rot** pot
You Lanarkshire **Ey**ot
You 6 over **par** shot
(for which a name there **is** not)
You under par **par**rot
You loaf full of **er**got
You counterfeit **in**got
You lazy of **Shal**lot
You 3 legg'd oce**l**ot
You leaky spi**g**ot
You Gerrymandered **bal**lot
You glamour red-**eye**shot
You rabid **fox**trot
You early shot **car**rot
(or anything that **has** shot)
You unlucky **mas**cot
You Pontious **Pil**ot
You believe in **Tar**ot
You are no **big** shot (!)
You fly Aerof**l**ot
And class you **have** not
You're the 13th **moon**shot.

===

120